LATE INTO THE NIGHT

FIELD TRANSLATION SERIES 21

LATE INTO THE NIGHT:

The Last Poems of Yannis Ritsos

Translated by Martin McKinsey

FIELD Translation Series 21
Oberlin College Press

Publication of this book was made possible by support
from the Ohio Arts Council.

Library of Congress Cataloging-in-Publication Data

Ritsos, Yannis (translations and introduction by Martin
    McKinsey)
  Late Into the Night: The Last Poems of Yannis Ritsos
  (The FIELD Translation Series v. 21)

LC: 95-067112
ISBN: 0-932440-70-3 (paperback)

These poems were published in Greek under the title *Arga, poli argá mésa sti níhta* © 1991 by Eri Ritsou and Kedros, Inc.

Acknowledgment is made to the following publications, where some of these translations first appeared:

Artful Dodge: "Sitting Out the Rain" and "What Cannot Be Weighed"

FIELD: "Evacuation," "The Trial," "Until One Night," "The Original Position," "Stages of Weariness," "Post Script," "Painting Stones," "Garden in Autumn," "People and Suitcases," "Not Quite," "Self-Knowledge," and "Closing Words"

Harvard Review: "In the Garden"

The Kenyon Review: "Perhaps," "Forgetfulness," and "Bitter Knowledge"

Partisan Review: "Another Summer" and "Minimal Harvest"

TriQuarterly, a publication of Northwestern University: "The Other Fear" and "On Silence"

Virginia Quarterly Review: "Hypothermia," "Tokens," "Pointless Lucidity," "Two in the Afternoon," and "Sparse Leavings"

Willow Springs: from "Ticks of the Clock"

CONTENTS

INTRODUCTION

To read Yannis Ritsos' *Late Into the Night* is to experience a curious inversion. It was written during the years 1987-1989, a time when most of us felt jubilant or at least relieved over *glasnost* and the end of the cold war. Ritsos had a drastically different response. For this Greek poet and lifelong Communist, who had spent years behind barbed wire for his revolutionary writings and activities, the end of Soviet-style Communism meant the end of a dream.

In 1949, while interned in the notorious Makrónissos camp for political prisoners, Ritsos had envisioned the socialist future as a city "off at the great crossroads . . . / lit by a thousand colored lights / where people greet you with a simple nod of the head." Throughout his creative life, even when his poetry had taken an inward and more questioning turn, Ritsos never lost his faith in the Marxist cause, in its rightness and its necessity. It was a conviction that glimmered in the margins of even his darkest poems. A poem from this volume, "The Original Position," registers his shock at the sudden collapse of the Eastern Bloc:

> Night after night he stayed awake following
> the progress of two opposing armies on the map
> in a perpetual, undeclared war. He made no secret
> of his preference for the side following the red line.

He took great pleasure in moving the red pins
deeper and deeper into black territory, until
he came to the edge of the map where there are
no more villages or cities or islands or oceans
or even names. Then he looked back, and saw
that the black line had reached its original position.
The room was thick with cigarette smoke,
and he felt every one of those pins sticking into his back,
though without causing him pain. He gets up,
opens the window. Looks down into the street.
Not a soul. Not one car or pedestrian. Just
the dead, frozen city, glittering into the distance.

Athens, 1-18-88

In the late 20th century, the utopian city whose "thousand colored lights" once lit up the horizon has been shouldered out by the cold, glittering reality of urban capitalism. It is as if the century's long struggle for social justice had never happened: out on the beach road, we are told in "Same as Ever," "a pack of feral dogs is still fighting over a bone."

The awareness of this irreversible loss permeates Ritsos' last work, though rarely as schematically as in the poem above. Usually it appears in fragments of allegory — the defeated mountain-climbers and drowned divers, the messengers who arrive (out of the future?) yet say nothing — that are embedded in a larger, more inclusive mosaic of loss.

For all their acute political sensitivity, the poems of *Late Into the Night* are anchored in the personal. Their subject, at the most immediate and experiential level, is old age and the nearness of death — the poems of a man approaching 80. Sometimes they open out onto the luminous, silent world of deep memory:

On the black and white tiles in the hallway
someone had left a basket of apples. The window
overlooked the sea. Five fishermen were carrying
a large dead shark. Blood
dribbled on the cart-track. When I went
into the dining room, on the sewing machine lay
a bunch of carrots. Oh forgotten years of childhood,
mindless years, hypnotized by sunlight. . . .

("Intimations")

More often, however, they document the emotional attrition, the frailty and fatigue:

At night,
houses and trees and people grow heavy and droop
beneath an insuperable weariness — a weariness
that fifty or so years ago
a tiny butterfly could have lifted on one wing.

("Stages of Weariness")

Late Into the Night is an honest record of a common mortal, and a major literary figure, coming to grips with personal extinction. It does not heroize or prettify the process. What sets the book apart from other works of old age is the way this essentially private experience intersects with the global — as encapsulated, with typical obliqueness, in the poem "Nothing":

> . . . . That night, we met the five
> mountain climbers on their way down,
> exhausted, carrying the handsome flag-bearer
> wrapped in a red blanket. At
> precisely that moment, the ship's whistle blew.

The two events — the fall of Soviet Communism and the approach of death — become metaphors for each other, mutually reflecting surfaces. It's often impossible to say where one leaves off and the other begins: They merge into a single grief.

What has always been most striking about Ritsos' poetry is its ability to grab the outside world, its politics and social epiphenomena, and make it into something interior and ontological. In these last poems, Ritsos located the death of the Soviet experiment (he would not have called it a failure) within himself, in his own imagination and his ailing body. It came as little surprise when he died in November 1990, at the age of 81.

Stylistically, the poems are not unlike Ritsos' previous "testimonies," as he calls his work in the short form. As in all his best work, they move restlessly between the lyric and the mundane, the visionary and the absurd. They are most successful at their most mysterious, when they both invite an allegorical reading and resist it. If the political backdrop gives them a more pointedly symbolic feel, the poet nevertheless leaves it to the reader to decide when a red cap is more than just a red cap.

Ritsos has always used a variety of mythical personas and other impersonations to distance himself and his readers from the subjective content of his verse — the result, in part, of a Marxist-inspired aesthetic. What is new about these poems is their aura of intimacy, the sense we have, through all the shifts of person and tense, that the voice we hear, the gaze we follow, is Ritsos' own:

> I checked my watch: two o'clock. Some skin divers
> were coming back from the water, still in their wetsuits.
> One of them, carrying blue fins and a large octopus,
> looked at me expectantly, as if he knew me. "Hello," he
>   said.
> "Hello," I said back, and felt like I should have said more.
>   ("Two in the Afternoon")

Read in sequence, with attention to their datelines — most from Ritsos' summer retreat in Karlóvasi, on the island of Samos — the poems chart an emotional movement through time. They respond to each other, and qualify each other (an effect somewhat lessened in this translation of about two thirds of the originals). "Bitter Knowledge," for instance, seems to be commenting on the previous night's work:

> I sweep the charred moth wings off the table
> from the night before, knowing only
> that all their weight is in their weightlessness.

At least within each of its sections (originally conceived as separate volumes), *Late Into the Night* reads more like a sequence than any work by Ritsos since *12 Poems for Cavafy* of 1963. Still, there is no mistaking the poems, with all their devious indirection, for journal entries or confessionalism. They unfold through a series of carefully orchestrated feints and retreats, as Ritsos' imagination revolves around the sorrows central to his life: the loss of friends and vitality, the loss of a future. He is being less than candid when he writes, in "Last-Minute Diversions," of burning the last mask.

Nevertheless, a deeply personal tone of voice prevails. As nowhere else in Ritsos' work, we seem to be overhearing the poet in dialogue with himself, as he takes stock, one last time, of his life and his world. He records the details of this still largely rustic world not for posterity but as an act of homage, part of the ritual of naming that was as close to the religious as his work ever got:

> . . . cicadas, olive trees, oleanders, wells,
> two black cows dreaming under the poplars,
> and out in the yellow field, a chunk of marble. . . .
>
> ("Homeland")

These tireless refigurings of the everyday give us, coinciden-
tally, a sharply-focused image of today's Greece, with its
tourists and deafening motorcycles, its terraced fields gone
to seed. For Ritsos, a Greece coming into its own as a full-
fledged member of the modern world was not an altogether
pretty sight. It replicated, on the local and cultural level, the
political homogenization overtaking the world at large. Oc-
casionally, the poems throw off glints of a nationalist senti-
ment that, given recent events in Bosnia-Herzagovina and
elsewhere, may make the reader squirm. But this merely
reminds us of how deeply enmeshed Communism has been,
in Greece and other parts of the developing world, with the
struggle for national autonomy and self-determination.

Mostly, however, *Late Into the Night* fixes its attention
on more immediate presences: the "simple, familiar objects,"
in sometimes unfamiliar roles, that have always been the
household gods of Ritsos' poetry. They have grown fewer
with the years, with the sensory impoverishment of age, but
have lost none of their talismanic intensity. Yet part of the
book's sadness comes from knowing that the traditional world
these objects evoked was quickly receding into the past.

That Ritsos was personally taking leave of this world, at the very moment of its passing, makes the disengagement doubly painful for the poet — and doubly poignant for the reader. In some not so very complicated way, Ritsos' leave-taking is our own.

I would like to thank Ninetta Makrinikola of Kedros Books and Karen Sabasteanski for their help and encouragement. This translation is dedicated to the memory of my father, T.W. McKinsey (1920-1990).

Martin McKinsey

I.

THE NEGATIVES OF SILENCE

1987

MISGUIDED PURSUITS

Hours of unintentional or intentional forgetfulness.
  Fatigue.
Close your eyes. What was the point of all those centuries
lying awake, following the flicker of lights
through the darkness, barely deciphering a window
repeated in miniature in the lens of a young boy's
bottleglass spectacles — a window supposedly open
to the miracle of the world? Who were you trying to fool?
Surely not yourself. Go on then — close your eyes.

Karlóvasi, 6-29-87

BACK THEN

At night, an echo of great and glorious days
reaches you still: houses, forests, ships ablaze,
horsemen racing to belfries or down into the plain,
others bringing in the dead, raising flags,
painting the moon's red crescent on walls. Now
a riderless horse-cart careens down the beach road
and the stray black dog stares into the river
as if it already knew everything we don't want to see.

Karlóvasi, 6-30-87

BITTER KNOWLEDGE

Stay in this sheltering half-light with folded hands.
There's nowhere for the lame night-watchman to sit.
The chairs were sold off two weeks ago. Out front,
they're hosing out some large barrels. Barges
lie beached in the harbor. The newscaster's voice
carries from across the street. I don't want to hear.
I sweep the charred moth wings off the table
from the night before, knowing only
that all their weight is in their weightlessness.

Karlóvasi, 6-30-87

FORGETFULNESS

The house with the wooden stairs and the orange trees
facing the blue mountain. Country smells
gently waft through the room. The two mirrors
reflect the singing of birds. But in the bedroom,
the house slippers of an old person
lie on the floor where they were dropped.
Thus, after dark, the dead return home
to retrieve something they left behind —
a scarf, a vest, a shirt, a pair of socks.
No doubt it's from forgetfulness or inattention
that they take something of ours, too. The next day,
the postman goes by without stopping.

Karlóvasi, 6-30-87

INTIMATIONS

On the black and white tiles in the hallway
someone had left a basket of apples. The window
overlooked the sea. Five fishermen were carrying
a large dead shark. Blood
dribbled on the cart-track. When I went
into the dining room, on the sewing machine lay
a bunch of carrots. Oh forgotten years of childhood,
mindless years, hypnotized by sunlight between
two unknowable miracles. The large book
on the straw chair in the garden was closed.

Karlóvasi, 7-2-87

THE UNINVITED

The afternoon gardens are a festival:
colorful beach-towels draped on flowering shrubs
hint, under the soughing of cicadas,
at naked young bodies, sun-bronzed flesh
flaked with glittering salt. But somehow
you sense that you are not invited
to these public festivities. So you sit
alone, waiting for night, hoping the stars
will resume, by means of secret signals,
your private sacraments, light-years away.

Karlóvasi, 7-2-87

CLOSING WORDS

The unhappy girl gnaws at her collar.
So long ago. Our mothers are dead.
A hen cackles in the rubble.
We had no answers. Later,
we stopped asking. Night was falling,
wind blowing. A straw hat tumbled
out of the stands of the empty Stadium. Below,
    in the river,
watersnakes and turtles roamed at will.
And maybe this would serve as closure
for a story already remote from us, strange.

Karlóvasi, 7-6-87

PERHAPS

It's quiet out tonight. At the window, motionless, the black
   swan
with glittering eyes. The clock has stopped. Your fingers
add up to ten. You can count on that. But the curtain's
   faded.
Red reverts to gray. Friends disappear.
The young dairyman got drafted. Maria got divorced. One
   by one
the portraits of the dead are stored in the basement
with the cockroaches and the rats. If, however, the woman
unbraids her hair in front of the mirror,
perhaps a thread of music will find its way from the other
   side.

Karlóvasi, 7-8-87

THE CRAZY

What lies we come up with to keep
our little place in the world. At night,
the traffic cops go home, shops close,
the stars grow bolder to the west. Later,
out in the muddy street, you hear
the neighborhood crazy with the red cap
singing something to himself, sadly —
a children's song infested with wrinkles.

Karlóvasi, 7-9-87

INCIDENT

A strange woman, distant, reserved,
as if she were secretly clenching a thermometer
under her arm, all the while knowing
she didn't really have a fever. Then
the big woman came in from next door holding
a leather belt. She showed it to the man
as if it had a special significance for him.
The man put the thermometer back in its case, took
the belt, cinched it around his waist. Immediately,
he realized he was a poet. He went into the hall
smiling magnanimously at the five statues.
One of them was missing its hands and penis.

Karlóvasi, 7-11-87

MINIMAL HARVEST

The morning glows with healing light, barrel-chested
    plane trees.
The sea glitters carelessly into the distance, complete in
    itself.
But the others — how will they survive on such a paltry
    allotment?
They who once in a dream saw mass marches, banners,
    chanting crowds,
who after so many years of preparation now feel
    themselves
wholly unprepared? They look across at the hillside, dark
    with pines.
With great diligence and keen attention they amass
    fleeting
impressions — hoping to make their own claim on the
    present.
A young girl comes up the hill carrying a basket of
    mulberries.
Leave it at that: the hill, the young girl, a basket of
    mulberries.

Karlóvasi, 7-11-87

HYPOTHERMIA

At night, large ships sail past
all lit up, furrowing the horizon with deep
presentiments of sorrow. How quiet it is
in the chambers of memory! The cheap hotel,
the iron bed-frame, the cigarette butts on the stairs,
an antique candlestick on the wash-stand.
When you looked out the window to the west,
there were stars in the small sky, and a bicycle
propped against a wall. The next morning,
it poured rain. You hadn't slept all night.
But still you lingered, hoping that Diotima
would show herself in the depths of the mirror.

Karlóvasi, 7-13-87

ESCAPE

Perhaps the description called for a certain dignity,
but who was up to it? They sat on the ground,
removed their shirts, avoided looking at each other.
One man drew a circle in the dirt. Another tried
playing knuckle-bones all by himself. A third
watched the clouds — how they fled. I pictured
a glass sitting on an empty table, out in the open.
It was enough. I used my empty pouch as a pillow,
and in the angled light of that glass I fell asleep.

Karlóvasi, 7-14-87

TOKENS

One by one the sleek bathers will leave.
The fiery autumn sunsets will linger on the sea,
with one sad skiff — and still
we put off the rain, the rampaging winds,
still we put off the inevitable (for how long?).
Already yellow leaves pile up on the garden benches.
Perhaps, uncelebrated on its hill, the chapel to the Holy
Trinity remembers us. Meanwhile, here in the house,
the floor is littered with summer sandals
and little Persephone's big blue towel.

Karlóvasi, 7-16-87

DENOUEMENT

Following their failed attempt on the summit, we met the
      mountain-climbers.
They carried a torn blanket, and a red hat. Wild goats
were climbing up into the carob trees. We had lost
our trust in events, in dreams. Foreign vessels
were unloading something, taking something on in lead
      containers.
No one knew what was happening. The newspapers looked
      elsewhere.
Then the huge bull lumbered onto the roof and devoured
      the flag.

Karlóvasi, 7-16-87

Vague promises — who made them? and when?
Others made by us (who to?). We're used to it.
We saw the mountains going by at dusk like overladen
      camels,
we saw the fawn in the moon, nothing
around a daisy. Rust from mothballed ships
dirties the virgin waters. And up the hill,
behind the dark, vertical cypresses,
a plume of smoke held still, trying to bestow
some nonexistent meaning on us and on the world.
Ah — to think that silent beauty no longer takes us in.

Karlóvasi, 7-18-87

CONVERSIONS

The Saturday night regulars arrived without saying a word.
It was the month of July. They sat outside the shabby cafe,
watching swallows etch icons on the gold leaf of sunset.
They regarded the stoplights and the gas stations
up and down the street, and the small whitewashed shrine
at the Levétsova-Sparta turnoff. We'd learned
how hard it is to convert
the negative into a positive. Then came the Stranger.
He sat down on the shore and started throwing
losing lottery tickets into the water, as if launching paper
        boats.

Karlóvasi, 7-18-87

HARSH NEWS

Across the sand of early evening flashes
the shadow of two gulls. What question wakes
in that forgotten depth, when a fluff of soft down
lands before a door for years locked shut?
From within comes the slow tread of the absent ones,
they who once looked in the large mirrors
and believed what they saw. Outside,
the old man selling newspapers in the street
hoarsely shouted the harsh news.
One hole. Two holes. Nobody is present.

Karlóvasi, 7-20-87

PILGRIMAGE

They journeyed for days on end. Their faith in the miracle
    never faltered.
It would come, at any moment it would come: around a
    bend in the road,
over this hill, or the next. They would see it with their own
    eyes,
proclaim it with their tongues, perhaps even hold in their
    hands
a piece of his golden tunic. At the start of the second
    month,
weariness overtook them. All ten lay on the ground
and instantly fell asleep. The moon rose above them —
detached, absorbed in its own sorrow. Then the great
    boulders
tumbled soundlessly into the great void. And they woke
    up.
All about them — absolute, blinding brightness. And no
    moon.

Karlóvasi, 7-21-87

HOMELAND

They left the dead down in the plain
along with their horses, the black dog. They'd hidden
the flags in the ancient caves. What we called *patrída*
was cicadas, olive trees, oleanders, wells,
two black cows dreaming under the poplars,
and out in the yellow field, a chunk of marble
and a white bird on one leg looking into the distance
at a point beyond memory or forgetfulness.
With a pinch of dirt, two kernels of corn, and a clove,
their aging mothers fixed them amulets
and watched them leave. At their backs,
the pregnant black ewe bleated through the night.

Karlóvasi, 7-21-87

HOUR OF ANONYMITY

A little boy climbed up the tall tree.
A bird flew in through the window.
The bus never showed.
Women opened striped parasols.
The men put on dark glasses.
Kids undressed right in the street.
Then came the blitz of yellow motorcycles.
And those who once gave names to mountains, birds, and
    other wildlife,
were left without names (and I among them)
in a marble landscape melted down in the sun.

Karlóvasi, 7-22-87

POST SCRIPT

Saying things over and over sapped them of meaning and
    color —
rocks, water, windows, the man with the old suitcase
outside the customshouse waiting, the big clock
striking eight p.m. and the boat nowhere in sight,
though its whistle already blew. Out on the pier,
the great crane rose among empty panniers like a cross.
Later, the stars came out over the slow, somnolent barges
and there, in the deserted plaza, at the foot of the heroes'
    memorial,
the four sailors deposited the body of the drowned diver.

Karlóvasi, 7-22-87

NOT QUITE

Through the open door, you see them:
two women — mother and daughter? — in black kerchiefs,
seated side by side on an old sofa. They don't move or talk.
A loaf of bread sits on the table in front of them.
A cat sleeps in the chair. Outdoors, the bay glitters,
the cicadas screech, scores of swallows write something
on the air — something finished yet incomplete.
But before I can say exactly what I mean,
the old woman gets up and shuts the door.

Karlóvasi, 7-25-87

ANOTHER SUMMER

These days of bright sunshine pull the plug on sorrow.
The houses scattered on the green hill gleam with
    whitewash.
And look — a roan horse grazing in the field. Out of
    summers past rises
a forgotten memory. Yes, the girl in the cornfield was real,
and that boy in the gold-dust of afternoon, waving
a red beach towel at a passing boat. *You* were real, too,
with your faith in music and nothing to your name
but what you gave away, and what you still might give.

Karlóvasi, 7-25-87

PEOPLE AND SUITCASES

Don't leave your wet towel on the table.
It's time to start straightening up.
In a month or so, another summer will be over.
What a sad demobilization, putting away bathing suits,
sunglasses, short-sleeves, sandals,
twilight colors on a luminous sea. Soon,
the outdoor cinemas will be closed, their chairs
stacked in a corner. The boats will sail
less often. Safely back home, the lovely tourist girls
will sit up late, shuffling through color glossies
of swimmers, fishermen, oarsmen — not us. Already,
up in the loft, our suitcases wait to find out
when we'll be leaving, where we're going this time,
and for how long. You also know that inside
those scuffed, hollow suitcases there's a bit of string,
a couple of rubber bands, and not a single flag.

Karlóvasi, 7-26-87

THE LATEST WORD

Time's running out. Strange messengers arrive
out of the mountains. They stop at the river,
take off their clothes, bathe themselves. Then,
at the first sign of nightfall, they go
back without leaving a message. The others
crouch in the moonlight. They can't decide
what road to take. Their fields untended,
corn ungathered. Then Vangélis appeared
out of nowhere, threw his pack on the ground,
and catching his breath said, "Old men, what
more are you waiting for? There *is* no other road."

Karlóvasi, 7-27-87

A PILLAR

Rocks and thorns and cicadas — everything bone-dry.
The wells and streams dry, the birds gone elsewhere.
The olive trees cling to a bit of green, the waves glitter
    blue.
At some point a boat shows up on the horizon. It doesn't
    stop.
Old people and babies die. Bedsheets scorch the skin. But
    night and day
that pillar just stood there, gleaming. So Thanásis said,
"I'm going to climb it, I'm going to shout up at God to
    make it rain."
He climbed it, and shouted. It didn't rain. Thanásis
fell off the pillar. He was buried the next day.

Karlóvasi, 7-27-87

WHAT CANNOT BE WEIGHED

Those who are left await their turn.
Mihális gone, Stratís gone, Melétis,
Sotíris gone at 40. The mule-drivers
come down from the villages, their carts
loaded up with watermelons. Right in the street,
they plop them on the scales and weigh them.
"Poor crop," they say — and the prices go up.
And old Státhis sits on his porch, oblivious,
gazing off at the ocean and chuckling to himself.
All this measuring and comparing — what's the use?
As if you could ever know the weight of things.
"Fresh watermelons," they shout, "ready for the knife!"
The mules doze in the heat, swishing their tails.

Karlóvasi, 7-28-87

TOPOGRAPHY

Donkeys, their hooves still caked in mud from the
    crossings,
come into town lugging huge baskets of tomatoes, eggplant
    and okra.
Some beat-up old farmtrucks come, too, with blaring
    loudspeakers
selling huge watermelons in the hot sun. Then come the
    fishermen
wandering the streets with a few sad-looking fry and
    sardines.
Cats dart through the weeds, windows fly open.
Ah, for a breath of *maístros!* Curious tales, secrets
with gaping holes, are going round the harbor; clothespins
nip at towels, shifts and underwear in the courtyards;
cicadas and sparrows keep up their chatter. Of course,
you find less superstition in the countryside these days. At
    night, however,
I often catch the old women flinging a bit of salt behind
    the door,
I catch you, too, carving something on the wall
to exorcise the evil on the other side of the wall.

Karlóvasi, 7-29-87

STRANGE DREAM

I don't know why — he says — but I keep having this
    dream:
a big, dirty fish market, littered with fish guts and
    dry scales.
Old men and women sit on the benches, squinty-eyed girls
    clutching
long rosaries that trail soundlessly across the dark tiles
in the half-light leaking from the dingy panes of glass
    overhead.
But the strangest part is, they're not selling fish, but parrots
in cages — weird-looking parrots, of all different colors.
One of them perched on my shoulder, put its beak to my
    ear and said, "Shit."

Karlóvasi, 7-29-87

TWO IN THE AFTERNOON

In the yellow field, a straw hat and a red cow.
A white horse switching greenflies with its tail.
I remembered the dead poet's cornfield, and sunflowers.
I checked my watch: two o'clock. Some skin divers
were coming back from the water, still in their wetsuits.
One of them, carrying his blue fins and a large octopus,
looked at me expectantly, as if he knew me. "Hello," he
        said.
"Hello," I said back, and felt like I should have said more.
Then a breeze came down off the mountain, the olive trees
shivered, the cicadas stopped. With a feeling of peace,
I stepped forward to stroke the white horse's mane.

Karlóvasi, 7-29-87

NOTE

The first notes for the collection *The Negatives of Silence* were taken in Athens, Kálamos, Diakoftó, Andravída, Kiparissía, and Andrítsena, from June 5, 1986, to June 27, 1987. First draft of the poems was written in Karlóvasi from June 29 to July 30, 1987, the second draft (the one here) in Karlóvasi from July 31 to August 25, 1987. As always, the poems bear the date of their first writing.

Y.R.

II.

THE BARE TREE

1987

USELESS KEYS

This far and no farther. There is no farther.
The local bus unloads foreign tourists,
foreign luggage, foreign sleeping bags.
You don't even recognize the suitcase
that once held something of yours —
a favorite blue shirt, that snapshot
of your first love. The books on the shelves
turn their backs, the heap of keys
on the table — you don't know
and don't care what locks they go to. . . .
This little silver one, for instance —
Ah, yes, it's to that jewelry box
full of diamonds, emeralds, sapphires,
a gold crucifix with three rubies,
that fell down the well years ago.
They drained the well, searched. They found
nothing, only rocks. Young Persephone,
it's said, took the rest with her underground.

Karlóvasi, 8-7-87

ON SILENCE

It is precisely the things you never said
that pumped blood into the words you did say, that hung
suspended in air, equivocal, opaque — notes
from some dark music out of the future. Now,
you have nothing to say because you have nothing to hide.
    Silence
muscles you out of things — so you eavesdrop
on the mating cry of motorcycles out on the coast road,
you hear the whistles of the *Samena,* the *Ikaros,* the
    Aegean
as they depart, night and day, in rough seas and calm,
their final destination that vast, unlighted anchorage.

Karlóvasi, 8-7-87

THE OTHER FEAR

They did well to battle the old fears, with heads unbowed.
Prison, torture, exile — the night before his execution,
     Yiórgos
wrote to his mother: "Don't cry," he said,
"I'll die standing up. Don't forget to say hello for me
to the mountains, the birds, the trees." Aléxis
carved a hammer and sickle on the wall of his cell,
then signed his name underneath. Others sang and danced
before the lowered barrels. They did well. But this fear
is silent, unbreathing, an invisible adversary.
It doesn't curse you or club you, doesn't pull a gun.
Invisible, it just waits. All you can do
is calmly and with some dignity lay out the clothes
for your last day: black shoes, black socks,
a black suit. But in the lapel a red carnation
in memory of those other days, those other, conquered
     fears.

Karlóvasi, 8-7-87

DEPLETION

The horses with their handsome riders are gone.
The houses in the village are empty. A few old men
sit on the low wall and watch the sunset.
What's there to say? The wine-jars and the moon
have been empty for years. The old men have forgotten
their olive trees, their vines, their grandchildren.
But sometimes at daybreak, in their sleep, they hear
the stars scratching on the wall with their nails,
searching for a treasure that's never been found.
When the old men wake up, they're more tired than ever.
They grasp their canes as if for support, or as if
to strike at some ancient enemy they can't see.

Karlóvasi, 8-8-87

THE STATUES AND US

The statues are so calm. The ravages of time
don't concern them. There go their hands,
their feet, their head — but they
persevere in their original uprightness.
Even flat on their backs, they smile,
or face down in the mud they turn
their backs on us, and on Time, as if
surrendering themselves to some infinite
act of love-making, while we look on,
unaccountably tired and depressed. Later,
we go back to our shabby hotel, draw
the blinds against the afternoon glare,
and sprawl naked on the lumpy bed, emulating
the placid immobility of the statues.

Karlóvasi, 8-9-87

FROM ANOTHER TIME

Strange — in that burnt shell of a house
the large mirror remained intact, and a glass bowl
with rotted apples. Through the gaping windows,
the sea glittered on and on, as if
nothing had happened. The dead were buried in a mass
    grave,
in the small cemetery on the hill. A week later,
the others returned. They came and stood at the door,
crossed themselves, then left again. The youngest sailor
lingered. He went inside, tripping over charred timbers,
and looking in the mirror, he saw the figure of Theódoros
    Kolokotrónis*
astride his horse, wearing his crested helmet, holding a
    huge clump
of black grapes, which he chewed up and swallowed one at
    a time.

Karlóvasi, 8-11-87

*Hero of the Greek war of independence.

GARDEN IN AUTUMN

They weren't waiting for anything, just sitting quietly
in the garden, their straw chairs soaking up the dampness
(already the first chill was in the air). They looked out at
the sea, the clouds, the hills, the old tanneries
long abandoned and half in ruins, like ancient temples.
Nearby, two yellow hens pecked at black watermelon seeds.
Off behind the cypresses, the fruit peddler cried
the last grapes; a boat's whistle blew in the distance.
The three old men looked at each other and slowly
nodded their heads, because they knew
it wasn't blowing for them. They had already left.

Karlóvasi, 8-15-87

SLUGGISHNESS

It's late, past midnight. There's no place to go.
The bars down at the harbor are closed. The sailors
have taken off their white uniforms and are probably
    asleep.
A few barges, heavy with their cargo of wood as if with
    child,
creep through the dark waters and the slivers of the moon's
broken window. 1:30, 2:00, a quarter past three —
the hours drag, and the smell of damp, fresh-cut timber
cannot erase the shadow looming in front of Customs,
where only yesterday handsome skin divers in their prime
beat the all-powerful octopus on the rocks
again and again, in a thick, semen-like liquid.

Karlóvasi 8-16-87

SPARSE LEAVINGS

Vineyards, olive groves, white houses strewn on the side of
    the hill,
swallows, sparrows, cicadas — they almost belonged to us
once. At night, the crickets lit up our sleep
with their small cries. Eléni went back to Sparta
years ago — left us here with a few robes of tattered
    gossamer,
a few empty perfume crystals. With their help,
we deluded ourselves for a while, in waves of nostalgia.
We deluded the others too; — no one noticed a thing.
The Dioscuri, of course, were turned into stars.
So we believed in our own metamorphosis. But now
the broken thermometer doesn't give any reading.
Only sometimes, in our sleepless nights, the beads of
    mercury scattered on the ground
wink at us, like make-believe stars.

Karlóvasi, 8-17-87

WORK TABLE

The table where you wrote your daily poems
is worm-eaten, bullet-riddled. At night,
the wind plays it like a flute, and sometimes,
in the small hours of morning, heavenly Urania comes
and lays her white handbag on the tabletop,
then her white gloves, her five bracelets.
She lies down beside you. You pretend to be asleep.
And who knows, maybe you really are asleep.

Karlóvasi, 8-20-87

SELF-KNOWLEDGE

He leaves sleep behind, and the road the moon paves
with thin gold leaf. He's on his own now,
here, in this little, this next-to-nothing,
with a walking stick and an empty basket. He sees
mountains, hovering in the mist. His loneliness
is weightless now, he could almost fly. But no.
He sits in a chair. Picks up an apple. Bites into it.
At last, he can read his proper name — in the teethmarks.

Karlóvasi, 8-27-87

SITTING OUT THE RAIN

The first rains are here. The wet horses
stand under the trees in their autumn dotage.
Their eyelids droop as they pretend to chew
a mouthful of dry grass. Maria wanted
to use her own comb on their wet manes. But
the last of the summer people were already leaving.
A hen clucked lewdly nearby. How sad it was watching
the hungry sparrows hop through the stripped vineyard,
the clouds changing shape overhead, flying apart despite
the crows like black tacks, holding them in place.
Thus, in a matter of hours, Maria grew old.

Karlóvasi 8-28-87

PAINTING STONES

To paint on stones — quiet, forgotten, taking
their mute dictation. Look: a young girl,
all innocence and beauty, her breasts bare. Her eyes
luminous with your own sorrow: that you never loved her.
And over here: the classical ephebe, his curls tied back
    with a ribbon,
his profile flawless. A discus-thrower, most likely,
or musician. But there was no room on the stone
to show the lyre, where it rested on his knee.
Late at night, however, long past midnight, you hear
that invisible lyre, playing something wonderful,
a poem you'll never write, while the ambulances
scream down your street transporting the 78 victims.

                              Karlóvasi, 8-29-87

NOTE

The Bare Tree was written in Karlóvasi, Samos, from August 7 to August 31, 1987. Successive revisions took place from September 14 to November 21. Final revision and rewrite, from November 23 to December 27, 1987.

Y.R.

III.

LATE INTO THE NIGHT

1988

INERTIA

In the bedroom, the woman with the black dog.
The elderly servant went down the hall carrying a lamp.
Not a breath of wind — yet the curtain stirred.
We'd given up hope of their return. Their clothes
had grown old on the hangers. That night,
we heard the messenger stop at our door.
He didn't knock, didn't say a word. The next day,
we found his gold-tipped cigarette butts in the garden.

Kálamos, 1-6-88

SAME AS EVER

Nothing's left in houses or trees. Birds
have nowhere to land. Street peddlers
march past all day. We know them by now:
imitation jewelry, synthetic cloth.
They leave after dark, their wares unsold. Nevertheless,
out on the beach road, when the lights come on,
a pack of feral dogs is still fighting over a bone.

Kálamos, 1-6-88

NOTHING

Fish-bones and cracked urchin-shells
on the big table under the trees.
A lonely transistor in the guardhouse.
When did they get here? When did they leave?
Who were they? That night, we met the five
mountain climbers on their way down,
exhausted, carrying the handsome flag-bearer
wrapped in a red blanket. At
precisely that moment, the ship's whistle blew.

Kálamos, 1-6-88

THE SOUND OF THE BELL

Daybreak — and our lamp still lit.
Ocher mixed with a bit of blue.
Gas-burner, coffee, the smell of staleness,
age. Playing cards everywhere,
ashtrays overflowing. Women, men,
gardens, books — here one minute,
then gone. Gone. And that tinkling
you heard right before dawn wasn't the mail,
just a sad little lamb being led off to slaughter.

Kálamos, 1-7-88

TRIFLES

Hair clips, belts, razors —
oh street-peddler, you'll never know
what your humble wares meant to me,
what balcony doors they've opened
onto the sea, what forests
shading me, statues loving me —
and now this little snail
with its two gelatinous horns
blithely navigates a leaf,
dreaming my dream.

Kálamos, 1-7-88

GOOD LUCK

Poplars, olive trees, fig trees,
eucalyptus; names, shapes, images,
statues abandoned in their loveliness,
an old bicycle, rusted out,
the dead boy's plastic boats —
you forget what they're used for,
you don't know who to leave them to.
So my friends, good-bye, and good luck.
Not one of night's stars is a lie.

Kálamos, 1-7-88

BALANCE

Two dead birds in the hunter's pouch.
I saw the blood on the rocks,
I saw the sorrow of the boat
disappearing over the horizon.
I waited till 7 p.m. Then came
the heavy rains and the wind.
One by one the musicians departed,
holding newspapers over their heads.
They left their instruments on the table.
At last I was free either to sleep or to fly.
Instead, I decided to put on one sock.
Now everything is in its natural place.

Kálamos, 1-8-88

LAST-MINUTE DIVERSIONS

The movement of the curtain cloaks the second face.
The floor is littered with pistachio shells
and three soft slippers — an old man's.
The red sweater thrown over the chair. Truly,
you have worn many masks in your time. Now
you toss them onto the fire one after the other
and enjoy watching them go up in flames,
the red glow flickering on your idle hands.

Kálamos, 1-8-88

THE NAILS

Who needs this, or that, or the other?
The dog died, then the horse.
Under the stairs — the empty bucket.
Fishermen go by crying their fish.
The house rings with absence,
and in the mirror, a pale crucified Christ
greedily clutches the two nails.

Kálamos, 1-9-88

EVACUATION

Houses empty out, little by little. Words, too.
This basket still had apples in it just yesterday.
The knife-grinder used to come by, sharpening old knives.
    Now
you stick your arm out the window, not to motion a cloud
    or a boat,
just to check the air outside, and your hand comes back
with the cold, corrosive touch of nothing there.

Kálamos, 1-9-88

NAUGHT

Tired faces, tired hands.
A tired memory. The desolation
when the hearing starts to go. Night
fell. Children grew up, left home.
You don't expect an answer. But then,
what was your question? All for naught,
those years you tortured yourself
trying to plaster a smile of approval
on your cardboard mask. Close your eyes.

Karlóvasi, 1-16-88

THE EVERLASTINGS

Last year, and the year before, and fifty years ago,
we read the same newspapers that are on the stands today,
and, who knows, maybe two centuries from now they'll be
    reading
the same ones: wars, floods, plagues. . . . A glass
falls and breaks. In the morning, the women
take the sheets out into the courtyard to air, along with
your crutches — because they too have grown so moldy
    and rotten
that from now on you'll have to hold them up, instead of
    the other way around.

Athens, 1-16-88

THE TRIAL

Some people hurried down the boulevard without
stopping to look in the shop windows. The others
were on their way back from the funeral, and tired out,
wearing overcoats that were much longer than usual.
In their pockets they still had an uneaten half
of dried rusk (the kind used at memorial services)
which they were waiting to throw away on the first
deserted street. Behind them, dressed in black,
came the mother, picking up the crumbs as if gathering
evidence for the great trial of those who survived.

Athens, 1-17-88

UNTIL ONE NIGHT

Aunt Marítsa and Aunt Katína, with their little hats,
their gold pins, their house chockablock with furniture,
their trunks full of embroidered double sheets,
their menagerie of brass kitchenware — Why did we
    collect it all, they'd say,
we can't even sit down in here. Nevertheless
they went on collecting — string,
clothespins, paper bags, while the roaches and the moth
rustled about their business. Until one night
the house caught fire. And those two willowy spinsters
ran into the street barefoot, half-undressed,
their long white nightgowns floating behind them,
and stood dumbfounded, trembling as they watched the
    fire,
each clutching a small black hat and nothing else.

Athens, 1-17-88

THE ORIGINAL POSITION

Night after night he stayed awake following
the progress of two opposing armies on the map
in a perpetual, undeclared war. He made no secret
of his preference for the side following the red line.
He took great pleasure in moving the red pins
deeper and deeper into black territory, until
he came to the edge of the map where there are
no more villages or cities or islands or oceans
or even names. Then he looked back, and saw
that the black line had reached its original position.
The room was thick with cigarette smoke,
and he felt every one of those pins sticking into his back,
though without causing him pain. He gets up,
opens the window. Looks down into the street.
Not a soul. Not one car or pedestrian. Just
the dead, frozen city, glittering into the distance.

Athens, 1-18-88

STAGES OF WEARINESS

The trainsmoke lifts gently into the red glow of evening.
An old woman sits in her doorway with a canary cage
listening to the blind man play his accordion on the steps
    of St. Varvára's.
We were out of reasons for today, for tomorrow. Things
resisted our names for them.
Stray dogs roam the neighborhood. At night,
houses and trees and people grow heavy and droop
beneath an insuperable weariness — a weariness
that fifty or so years ago
a tiny butterfly could have lifted on one wing.

                                            Athens, 1-19-88

IN THE GARDEN

The gardener spent little time on the flowers.
The fruit trees were a different story. He wore
a fraying straw hat like a stolen halo. Each afternoon,
a group of boys and girls gathers under the tree
with a very chic-looking actor. They're rehearsing
some lighthearted play — most likely a pastoral.
The gardener discreetly gathers up his tools
and retires to his wooden hut deep in the ivy
for his midday rest. And I am able to confirm
(thanks, perhaps, to the cries of the young actors)
that in his sleep the gardener takes great pleasure
        attempting
to prune, with long clippers, the watery branches
of the never-silent fountain. In this way,
I too regain a portion of ephemeral immortality.

Athens, 1-20-88

INNOCENCE

The flowershop, the fruitseller, the bakery, the grocer's,
the butcher's farther on. A woman goes by carrying
an enormous head of lettuce. The policeman watches her.
But how can I establish *my* innocence, with night
stealing in so quickly to hide me? The stars
tactfully divert our attention. All
I ever dreamed of was a single impossible leaf
from that enormous head of lettuce in the sad woman's
      hands.

Athens, 1-20-88

CHANGES

Those who left were like family. We missed them.
The ones who came back were complete strangers.
They didn't use to wear glasses. Now they do.
How can we be sure they have eyes underneath?
We'd have to look at them in their sleep,
when their suitcases, lying open in the hall,
exhale the alien odor of new underwear,
and out in the street the floodlight comes on,
shining into the doorways of the closed shops
and the impenetrable lies open before you, now
that you have nothing left to buy or to sell.

Athens, 1-23-88

TONIGHT

Tonight, the once compliant dark gave us a scare.
The trees were frozen in threatening postures.
The last few stars, which we'd thought safe,
were looted and empty. A woman
threw a ceramic vase out the window.
The sound of it breaking reached the other side
wholly unmixed with music. The second man
came out of the door below clutching a large
bird to his torso, probably an ostrich.
Then its cry declared it to be a peacock.
Later, after midnight, the railway strike began,
and all those waiting at the train stations
hoisted their baskets, their blankets, their suitcases, boxes,
and embarked on the silent march of captives
who don't know where they're being led, or by whom.

Athens, 1-23-88

TRAFFIC

A man with a limp goes by carrying a cello without a case.
Everyone stares. The butcher's parrot squawks,
"Your hat, sir, your hat" — and, sure enough,
the man takes off his hat. The traffic cop
gesticulates angrily: The light is red,
everything must stop — wheels, feet, buying,
selling, the newspapers, the —
"Excuse me, did you say something?" "No, no, thank you."

Athens, 1-25-88

PRIVILEGED

A quiet winter afternoon: Two soldiers on leave
stroll along the waterfront. A woman in makeup
stands watching the ships, the cranes, the stevedores,
the single gull over the masts. The bicyclist
stops in front of the shipping agency. He unloads
a stack of old newspapers. A small plaster nude
watches you from the window of the stationer's. And you
feel privileged and flattered
by the favor statues have always shown you,
and by their confidences.
So you buy a handful of roasted pumpkin seeds
and throw them into the water one at a time, knowing
that little statue in the stationer's is watching.

Athens, 1-27-88

WRONG NUMBER

Disclaimers, denials, re-evaluations. Nothing.
Now you sit in a soft cloud, an old chair,
examining your fingertips, cigarette-yellow.
Numbers, events elude you. Losses and gains
(what gains?) don't concern you. You've lost
your old friends' addresses. And if some night
your telephone rings, as if from very far off
a stranger's voice says: "Sorry. Wrong number."

Athens, 2-2-88

A FLOWERSHOP

He spent all his worldly goods. He even spent
all his secrets on ambiguous words. He's used up
his last reserves of heaven in silent rituals,
in mock symposia with empty cups, in music
sans instruments. Now he is silent. Nevertheless,
he knows that at the corner of Kóraka and Papanastasíou
that sad little flowershop is still in business,
and the strange thing is, there are people,
poor people most likely, who still buy flowers.

Athens, 2-5-88

AND THE POEM

How lovely the trees are, blanketing the hills.
May's turned everything green. Behind the trees,
the little white houses are discussing something
tranquil and white — the arrival of ships,
the arrival of vacationers, birds, love-affairs.
"But I," he said, "am leaving." And the poem
with a cross of wax sealing shut its mouth.

Kálamos, 5-2-88

TURNED SOIL

There are still birds. They even sing.
There are trees, and the sea in its innocence.
The vinestocks are green again. Olives
swell on the branch. And the air is filled
with the rich smell of turned earth. You notice
the color of the mountains — almost blue. You try
to answer the birds, but nothing comes. Your eyes
keep going back to the turned soil, where it waits
for the new shoots, the rosebushes and the dead.

Kálamos, 5-2-88

THE BLACK BOAT

The old man sits in his doorway. It's night-time,
he's alone. In his hand, an apple. The others
left their lives to the stars' jurisdiction.
What can he tell them? Night is night.
We don't even know what comes next. The moon
amuses itself halfheartedly, endlessly
shimmering on the sea. But in the heart
of all that brightness, there is no mistaking
the black boat with its shadowy oarsman
slowly drawing away from shore.

Athens, 4-5-88

NOTE

The poems in *Late Into the Night* were written in Athens and Kálamos from January 1 to May 4, 1988. They were reworked and rewritten in Karlóvasi, Samos, from July 14 to 29, 1988. Fourteen poems were eliminated.

Y.R.

IV.

TICKS OF THE CLOCK

1988-1989

1.

Last night, the old blind man
passed me on the street.
He was holding a daisy —
my closing argument.

2.

Even the ash pan
with evening coming on
sometimes looks in the mirror.
Faces have more color then.

3.

In the center of the great hall,
a large table
with an empty cello case on top.
Remember?

4.

As she was coming down the stairs,
a rose fell from her hair.
I didn't pick it up.

5.

You're better off saying nothing.
Say "tomorrow"
and you'd be lying.
Night can't hide you.

Karlóvasi, 8-20-88

7.

This year, the sunflowers
don't turn toward the sun.
They bow their heads,
staring at the dry ground.

8.

Wonder what the birds think
in early autumn
when the wheelbarrow
with the empty flowerpots
is riveted to its shadow
and the bare stones
have the first and last word.

9.

The white feather
of a migratory bird
landed in the stickers.
The least of worlds —
the whole world.

10.

Some left by boat,
some by train.
The old lady stayed behind
with her distaff

and a clay jug.
The map on the wall is blank.

12.

Yesterday's soldiers are old now.
Words, too, are dying out.
On the table, a lone egg.

13.

The stones you painted
 — pretty faces and bodies —
leave you cold.
Smoke rising from a cigarette
left burning in an ashtray
is smoke from a hearth
on some lost Ithaca — with Penelope
sitting at her loom,
dead.

14.

Most of the gold coins
you hid in cracks in the wall.

Who knows, maybe they'll find them
when they tear down the house.

16.

They lay the drowned man on the dock.
He was young, good-looking.
The watch on his left wrist
was still ticking.

20.

If I told you lies,
it wasn't to deceive you
only to protect you
from your shadow.

21.

All his gold medals
hanging on the wall,
and him underground
with two gold teeth.

23.

The door opened by itself.
No one there.
It's time you learned
to stop waiting.

24.

One stone atop the other:
he's not building a house.
One word after the other —
only words, not a poem.

28.

Once you owned a horse so white.
Now its harness
is around your neck.
Where is it taking you?

29.

These simple, familiar objects
became his friends.
They grew to trust him.
Now he sits with them in silence
and lights a cigarette — his only star.

Athens, 9-28-88

35.

He holds the wind's hand.
Together, they can go anywhere.
They don't. Instead, they sit
without moving or speaking,
each hiding the other.

10-1-88

37.

Words fade with the years.
The word *mother* remains
with a veiled smile
and a black kerchief.

38.

Your wings have grown too big.
Better have them trimmed
at the corner barbershop.
Just don't look in the mirror.

40.

The spermaceti slowly melts,
dripping wax on my papers.
If only it would blot out
the black words.

41.

He hasn't laid down arms. He wants to oppose
something beautiful to advancing night.
But each lovely thing is transparent,
on the other side he can always see
the meadow of asphodel.

42.

Before I could count to ten
on my fingers,
night fell —
leaving us
without dreams, bread.

10-4-88

43.

Once again he tried to climb
the great stairs.
He didn't make it.
He came back down, propped
on his fatigue.

44.

A time of ellipses,
of ambiguous smiles.
The wine's gone flat
in the eleven glasses.
The twelfth glass is empty.

Athens, 10-5-88

49.

Gone are the birds, the leaves, the stars.
Now,
what kind of voyage can you take
in a drop
of water?

10-6-88

51.

Once, the moon shielded you
from its own melancholy.
Now it simply turns away,
impassive in its longevity,
aloof in its silence,
desolate.

10-7-88

52.

No way forward.
If you could just go back,
maybe you'd find

a sparrow waiting
in the old garden.

10-12-88

56.

You temporize with lyric contrivances.
You look at yourself in the water, and dream.
Well, at least you've still got your looks.
Those wrinkles on your high forehead
are the reflection of the water,
trembling with emotion.

57.

With the vast assurance of one
who has given up hope,
he hides behind his smile.
He gives children candy
and old men balloons.

59.

Why try to see any farther?
The three mistresses of deceit

keep their faces half hid
behind their fans.

61.

Where did those days go?
Remember your little chats
with a sparrow, or with a small moon
that wrote your name on the ripples
a thousand times, and you
recognized it, and were it?

10-15-88

65.

The stovepipe rusted,
the mirror cracked. Who's that
sleeping in our bed,
a black bird
perched on his forehead?

10-16-88

69.

Across the street, the facades
are bright with sun.
Kids play in the schoolyard.
The shadow of a low-flying plane
flashes over the terrace,
over two doves as they kiss.
And you, alone with your blank pages.

10-20-88

70.

The mirror once aglow
with beautiful women
is blind now. In the hall,
lying where it fell on the rug,
the silver candlestick has gone out.

71.

Our windows no longer usher in
morning landscapes, starry night skies.
Now there's only blackness,

bandaged from top to bottom
with wide strips of gauze.

10-21-88

73.

What is white, is empty.
I write a word on a blank
sheet of paper — a hole
in emptiness. Through the hole
I see vehicles going past,
and the young flower-girl laying
small bouquets of jasmine
on the tables of working-class cafes.

74.

The sick tightrope walker
tries to maintain his balance
by keeping strict account of each
little wavering. Plus the four
windows facing the airshaft.

76.

The sound of horses
galloping through the night.
I opened the window.
Endless stars.
If I whistle, you'll come.

10-22-88

77.

Rain all day.
Kids stand at the bus stops
getting drenched.
And you at your window —
doing your best to alchemize
raindrop
into diamond.

78.

Back then — now that was cold.
No heat, no cigarettes.
So they struck a match,

set their manuscripts on fire.
Illuminating their deaths.

10-23-88

79.

Mothballs of autumn fill the house.
Rain plinks on the hoods of taxis.
The old weather vanes in poems point
at nothing, and under the cypresses
the *korae* stand waiting — marble
streaked with tears.

11-27-88

80.

No longer touched by events
or dreams,
he takes one shoe off,
leaves the other on.
He lies in bed
feigning sleep,
an unlit cigarette in his mouth.

12-20-88

81.

Over time, the names for things
no longer fit. Cigarette smoke
fills the house. Nicotine
poisons the lip of silence.
Tomorrow — must buy umbrella.

12-20-88

82.

We go back to what we abandoned,
what abandoned us. In our hands,
a mass of keys that will open neither
drawer or suitcase or door —
we jangle them together and smile
having no one left to fool —
not even ourselves.

1-1-89

NOTE

The first five sections of *Ticks of the Clock* were written in Karlóvasi, Samos, on 8-20-88. The remainder were written in Athens from 9-28-88 to 1-1-89. All were reworked and rewritten in Karlóvasi during July 1989.

Y.R.

A Poem from the Unfinished Volume

BOAT WHISTLES

1989

THE LAST SUMMER

Farewell colors of evening . . . . Time to pack
our three suitcases: books, papers, shirts . . . .
Don't forget the pink dress you looked so nice in,
even if you won't be wearing it this winter.
Meanwhile, in the few days left, I'll revise
the lines I wrote in July and August —
though I can't help thinking that I've added
nothing, have in fact subtracted far too much,
because what glimmers through those lines
is a lurking suspicion that this summer,
with its cicadas, its trees, its ocean,
its boat whistles blowing in glorious sunsets,
its caiques bobbing under moonlit balconies,
its feigned compassion — will be my last.

Karlóvasi, 9-3-88